I SPY
DIY STYLE

I SPY DIY STYLE

Find Fashion You **Love** and **Do It Yourself**

JENNI RADOSEVICH

POTTER
CRAFT

NEW YORK

Published in the United States by Potter Craft,
an imprint of the Crown Publishing Group,
a division of Random House, Inc., New York.
www.pottercraft.com
www.crownpublishing.com

POTTER CRAFT and colophon is a registered
trademark of Random House, Inc.

Library of Congress Cataloging-in-Publication Data

Radosevich, Jenni.
 DIY style : find fashion you love and do it yourself
 / Jenni Radosevich.
    p. cm.
 ISBN 978-0-307-58714-5 (pbk.)
 1. Dress accessories. 2. Handicraft. I. Title. II. Title: Do it
yourself style.
 TT649.8.R33 2012
 646'.3--dc23
                         2011034318

ISBN 978-0-307-58714-5
eISBN 978-0-307-58715-2
Printed in China

Design by Jenny Kraemer and Jenni Radosevich
Photography by Jamie Beck
Step-by-step photography by Jenni Radosevich

Cover design by Jenny Kraemer
Cover photography by Jamie Beck

10 9 8 7 6 5 4 3 2 1
First Edition

To Mom,
for listening to all my ideas,
supporting every creative
endeavor, never questioning
my fashion choices, and believing
in me since day one. Thank you
for always encouraging me
to be absolutely Jenni.

 # CONTENTS

ONE

18 ## RED CARPET READY

TWO

48 ## RIGHT FROM THE RUNWAY

INTRODUCTION

Trends come and go quicker than subway cars, and many times that must-have look can leave you with maxed-out credit cards. I say: "Find fashion you love and do it yourself!" Instead of breaking the bank for the trend du jour, grab some simple supplies and re-create it for less. You'll be amazed at what you can do with a few buttons, some fabric paint, or a piece of ribbon.

My love for DIY style started at a young age with an obsession for fashion magazines. Torn-out pages covered my walls and ceiling, and a collection of issues was stacked high in my closet. I kept a box labeled "inspiration" in my bedroom filled with tear sheets of the designer looks I adored and dreamed of imitating. High fashion wasn't something I could always afford, much less find, in Midwestern department stores, so I began to shop at thrift stores, sew, and embellish my own versions of the chic pieces I coveted. My first "custom creations" weren't always perfect: dresses from sewing classes were often a little lopsided; clothes I "borrowed" from my mom's wardrobe were too big; and my tie-dye/puffy paint phase was a little too, well, bright. Over the years, through trial and error, I learned a few clever tricks and techniques to make clothes and accessories that I loved—and that got me many compliments. I was ecstatic over the response I received when I confessed that I made it myself!

My fascination with fashion and magazines eventually turned into a career. Living in New York and working at *InStyle* magazine, I am surrounded by the same type of breathtaking designs I idolized as a youngster. The only thing that hasn't changed is that many of these fashions are still out of my price range. To remedy that, I still turn to my trusty glue gun, needle and thread, and jewelry pliers to re-create—in an affordable way—some of the gorgeous styles I see in the magazines and on the runway.

I always include DIY pieces in my outfits, and it is gratifying when coworkers take notice. *InStyle* asked me to do a "Personalize Your Clothing" story in one issue, and the reaction was overwhelming. From there, my website, I Spy DIY (ispy-diy.com), and a monthly do-it-yourself fashion column in the magazine were born. Being able to connect with others who share my passion for budget-friendly fashion has been absolutely amazing. Now, when I am stopped on the street or at a party, and am asked about a piece I made, I love sharing how you don't have to spend a fortune, but can easily do it yourself.

I Spy DIY Style is a go-to guide for girls who want to "get the look" on a budget. I've scoured the fashion landscape to bring you the most stylish DIY ideas. Red carpet celebs, designer runway looks, and classic iconic styles are my inspiration. I've taken my favorite clothing and accessory trends and turned each into a simple, step-by-step, do-it-yourself project. If you are looking to give clothing in your wardrobe new life, I have also included easy projects to refashion basics, such as a tank top, black flats, and a button-down shirt (pages 114, 122, 138). Top designers, including Erin Fetherston, Rebecca Minkoff, and Rachel Roy, contribute ideas on how to put a personal spin on what you wear; *InStyle* Fashion Directors share tips on making style your own; and fashion and DIY bloggers model each project and spill some of their best-kept secrets. And because this is all about upping your individual style, remember that the projects in the book can be customized in endless ways. Have fun and feel free to improvise. Once you get the techniques down, I have no doubt you'll be spotting and creating your own DIY style in no time!

"I think having personal style is so important for girls. **Embellishing** lets you turn something that was someone else's into something that's your own and to really identify who you are and **showcase** your personality to those around you. Personally, I'm a fan of studding, so I love it when I can add a little more to my own bags."

—REBECCA MINKOFF, HANDBAG AND FASHION DESIGNER

5 REASONS TO DIY YOUR STYLE

DIY style is not just about re-creating a look; it's about putting a **personal touch** on what you wear and, in the truest sense, making the trend your own.

1

2

It gives you a chance to **breathe new life** into something that you might otherwise send to the donation bin. A little embellishment, a few strategic snips, or some simple sewing can give your piece a much-needed makeover.

3

It makes you think more **creatively**. Dollar stores, flea markets, and hardware stores become treasure troves. Copper piping becomes a Cynthia Rowley–inspired necklace (page 64), a place mat is transformed into a nautical clutch (page 92), and an elegant ribbon can turn a basic jacket into a Coco Chanel-esque classic (page 82).

4

DIY is a great way to **try out a trend** without spending a lot of money. Invest in basics, and accessorize them with **affordable** and of-the-moment projects.

5

When a project turns out the way you envisioned, the sense of **accomplishment** is incredible, and the first compliment you receive will leave you beaming.

How to
DIY

DIY style is all about experimentation and creativity so
there are no set rules, but
before you dive into making
wearable projects, there
are a few basic materials
and words of advice that
will help ensure success.

Scissors

Glue

Jewelry pliers

Assorted beads, buttons, and other trim embellishments

WHAT YOU'LL NEED

The projects in this book don't require many supplies, but here is a list of some of the basic tools and supplies to get you started.

Paint

Findings

Needle and thread

Masking tape

Permanent markers, such as Sharpies

LOOK FOR:

Insider Tips: Styling ideas from fashion's finest, including top fashion bloggers, stylists, and designers.

Project Tips: Advice on where to shop for supplies and how to perfect your DIY techniques.

My Tips: Ways to put a personal twist on your projects, and how I'd wear the final look.

Fun Ideas and Alternative Projects

TIPS FOR SUCCESSFUL DIY

After years of trial and error, I've discovered a few tricks of the trade worth knowing before you heat up a glue gun or start to snip.

💡 Overbuy

When getting materials for a project it is always better to buy more, for three reasons:

1. Extra supplies give you a cushion for experimentation or mistakes.
2. It is always a letdown to run out of materials before finishing, and a project can look slapdash if you stretch what you did buy.
3. You can use the extras to build your craft closet!

💡 Go Thrift

Buy clothes for DIY projects from your local secondhand store. This way you can try a technique on an inexpensive piece of clothing instead of a more costly item from your wardrobe.

💡 Keep It Tidy

1. To prevent rope or braided trims from unraveling, wrap a piece of tape around the area you would like to cut. Using sharp scissors, cut in the middle of the tape. This will keep the piece you are using and the excess from coming apart.
2. Keep the edges of your ribbon from fraying by burning the ends with a lighter. Quickly move the lighter back and forth over each end to avoid burning it unevenly.
3. Reinforce your knots by dabbing a bit of superglue on them after tying.

💡 Paint Properly

When spray-painting:

1. Hold the nozzle 6 inches (15cm) away from the item you are painting and cover it with a thin coat. Let it dry, then spray a second coat, and repeat until it's completely covered. Paint will just run off the item and dry unevenly if you apply too thick of a coat.
2. Wear plastic gloves. More often then not, the paint will not only cover the intended item but also a handful of your digits.

When using fabric paint:

After decorating your clothing with fabric paint, let the garment dry fully, then turn it inside out and iron on medium heat. This will lock the paint to the material so it does not run in the wash.

💡 DIY Care Instructions

1. Dry-clean or hand-wash the clothing you embellish; some glues will not hold up in the wash.
2. Keep extra embellishments after finishing a project, so if a bead falls off or piece of ribbon comes loose, you can do a quick touch-up.
3. It is exciting to wear your latest DIY project, but to avoid a wardrobe malfunction, make sure to give the glue time to set, and the paint time to dry, before heading out the door.

💡 Make It Your Own!

Try new color combinations, or use the techniques on different garments than suggested. Just remember: It is all about being creative, so take the guidelines I give you and add your own personal touches.

INSIDER
SECRETS

I asked designers and DIYers for some of their best-kept tips, and uncovered some fantastic advice for anyone looking to do it yourself.

"A little hot glue goes a *very* long way."

—JESSICA QUIRK, AUTHOR OF *WHAT I WORE*, WWW. WHATIWORE. TUMBLR.COM

"Don't be afraid to get dirty, and remember practice makes perfect. Aim to feel comfortable with a new process before cutting into, painting, sewing, or altering a piece of clothing you love."

—ALISON DAHL, FASHION DESIGNER AND CREATIVE WWW.DIRECTOR OF BURDASTYLE.COM

STAY ORGANIZED

"Keep your supplies as organized as possible. Invest in jewelry boxes to separate bits and pieces, designate a shelf for bigger items, and neatly hang up or fold your fabric. You will be surprised at how much more room there is for creativity when you can actually see everything!"

—KIRSTEN NUNEZ, DIY BLOGGER, WWW.STUDS-AND-PEARLS.COM

"DIY projects are always easier if you have basic materials and tools on hand. Designate a couple of desk drawers or a cabinet for common DIY supplies like jewelry pliers, jump rings, grosgrain ribbon, studs, scissors, etc., so you always have something on hand when inspiration hits."

—KEIKO GROVES, DESIGNER OF POSTLAPSARIA AND FASHION BLOGGER, WWW.KEIKOLYNN.COM

"I find that some of the best DIY materials are things that I already have in my own closet! Whether it's an old necklace I can add paint to for a colorful statement necklace or a pillowcase I can morph into a fancy skirt, sometimes all you need is a little creativity to update an outdated look!"

—KRISTEN TURNER, DIY BLOGGER, WWW.GLITTERNGLUE.COM

DIY CHECKLIST

Buy a sewing machine. They're worth their weight in gold and will last forever.

Make time. A lot of people tell me that they never have any time to do DIY, so set aside a weekend every month to get creative. Better yet, invite some friends over so it's a fun and social experience.

Catalog your inspiration. Keep a journal or create a blog to store all your inspiration for DIY projects. That way, when you get a spare moment to make something you will already have some ideas.

Don't hold back. If you see something you like on the runway, ask yourself whether it would be possible to make it, think about the materials you'll need, and get to it! You'll be very happy with the result, I promise.

—GENEVA VANDERZEIL, DIY BLOGGER, WWW.APAIR-ANDASPARE.BLOGSPOT.COM

"Test things before you go right to the pieces you love. You don't want to ruin something without giving it a try first! And play dress-up *every* day!!"

—GRETCHEN JONES, FASHION DESIGNER AND *PROJECT RUNWAY* SEASON 8 WINNER

ONE

RED CARPET READY

Working at a fashion magazine, I spend a lot of time studying celebrity style (something I always consider a perk). From the red carpet at the Oscars, to movie premieres, and other glam events, I am fascinated by what my favorite celebs show up wearing, how their outfits are put together, and what new trends pop up. I especially enjoy following celebrities who like to **reinvent their look**, most likely because I often do the same. Drew Barrymore's willingness to **experiment** with everything from stripes to sparkle to eclectic pieces makes her a perfect candidate to inspire your next project. After spotting her photographed wearing a pair of **embellished earrings**, I couldn't help but take notice and make my own version (page 28). Obsessed with a grommet and woven leather dress Kate Bosworth wore, I replicated the look on a piece from my closet (page 24). Kate's stylist, Cher Coulter, offers some tips on what to wear with it. Pay attention to what the A-listers wear, and you might find some great DIYs that will have you sporting your own superstar charm.

PINK FEATHER EARRINGS

Inspired by Gwyneth Paltrow

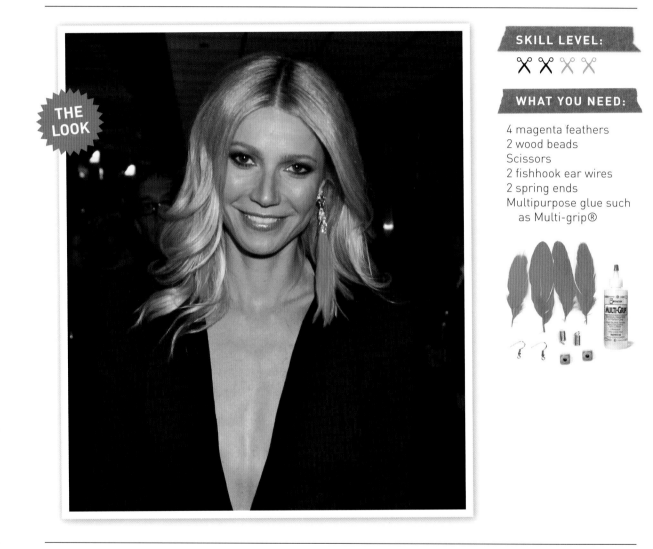

THE LOOK

SKILL LEVEL:

✂ ✂ ✂ ✂

WHAT YOU NEED:

4 magenta feathers
2 wood beads
Scissors
2 fishhook ear wires
2 spring ends
Multipurpose glue such
  as Multi-grip®

BOLD FEATHER EARRINGS are the perfect piece of jewelry to wear with a flowing dress for a bohemian look, or to make a bold statement with a basic black ensemble the way Gwyneth did. Hearts will flutter when friends spy this eye-catching accessory.

1. Line up the quill ends of two of the feathers.

2. Thread one of the wood beads on the two feather ends and then snip off the ends, leaving ½" (13mm).

3. Dab a little glue onto the feather end and insert into the spring end.

4. Connect the fish-hook ear wire to a spring end.

5. Repeat to make a pair and let both dry for 24 hours.

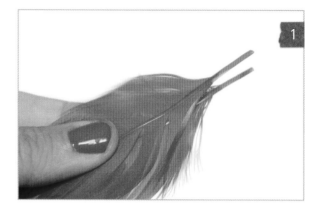

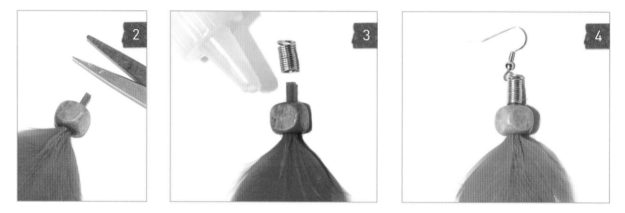

"These remind me of Blondie and '80s glam rock. I'd pair them with a black dress so they really pop, and paint my lips hot pink to match."

—ALISON DAHL, DESIGNER AND CREATIVE DIRECTOR OF WWW.BURDASTYLE.COM

GROMMET-THREADED DRESS

Inspired by Kate Bosworth

THE LOOK

SKILL LEVEL:

✗ ✗ ✗ ✗

WHAT YOU NEED:

Cotton dress
Forty ½" (13mm)
   grommets and
   washers (buy a kit
   including setting tools)
Marker
Hammer
Scissors
2 yd (183cm) thin
   leather rope

ONE OF MY FAVORITE STYLE STARS, Kate Bosworth looks effortless in a minimalist neutral-colored dress accented with a woven waistline. Re-create this chic look with leather rope, grommets, and a little bit of hammering.

"I paired it with a large statement JewelMint piece because her dress had a slight sixties edge to it, and was the perfect canvas for a bright fun necklace. I would also add a simple cream-colored bag with no hardware so it doesn't compete with the waistline. Wear it with a wooden heel sandal or a simple nude round-toe pump."

—CHER COULTER, KATE BOSWORTH STYLIST AND CO-DESIGNER OF JEWELMINT

1. Fold your dress in half, and lay down the grommet tops in a straight line, evenly spaced across the width of the dress.

2. With the marker, mark the middle of each grommet with a dot.

3. Using your scissors, snip a small hole in each dot.

4. Turn the dress inside out. Place a grommet on one side of the hole (right side of dress), and the washer on the other side (wrong side of dress). Place the setting tool on top of the grommet and washer, then hit with the hammer multiple times until secure.

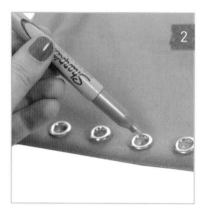

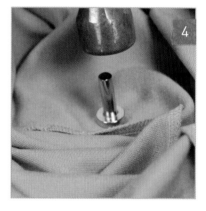

5. Repeat across the dress on each marked hole. Then create a second line of grommets below the first.

6. After all the grommets are secured, weave your leather rope through them, crossing the rope after every other set of grommets to create a crisscross pattern.

7. When you reach the end of the dress, lay it flat, then tie the rope ends and cut off any excess.

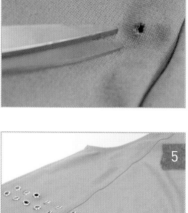

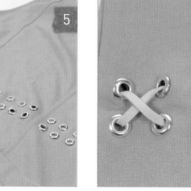

CHER COULTER'S STYLE TIPS

1 Transform a look by **layering pieces of jewelry**; it gives confidence and personality to any boring look.

2 **Rip apart** clothes you thrifted and turn them into something else.

3 Use earrings as pins or **necklaces as belts** to give you a great fashion twist.

Add a funky necklace to this dress like Kate, or let the embellishment make the statement and play down the jewelry with a simple silver bracelet.

HEMP HOOP EARRINGS

Inspired by Drew Barrymore

THE LOOK

SKILL LEVEL:

✂ ✂ ✂ ✂

WHAT YOU NEED:

1 pair of large hoop
   earrings
1 yd (91cm) each
   thin hemp rope
   in three colors
10 wooden beads
   in two sizes
Superglue

AFTER YEARS IN THE SPOTLIGHT, Drew Barrymore continues to reinvent her style. She looked spot-on at this movie premiere, sporting multicolored earrings with her evening attire. Drew was seen wearing these versatile hoops several times, dressing them up, then going more casual with slacks and a sparkly top.

1. Holding all three colors of hemp together, tie a knot on the end of one hoop earring.

2. Wrap one color of hemp rope around the earring and the other two hemp strands. Alternate with the other colors.

3. Thread a bead onto the earring over the hemp strands.

4. Repeat steps 2 and 3, alternating colors and beads in the pattern you desire.

5. Tie the rope in a knot when you reach the end of the hoop earring.

6. Trim the ends and secure the knot with superglue. Let dry for 5 minutes. Repeat steps 1 through 6 for the other hoop.

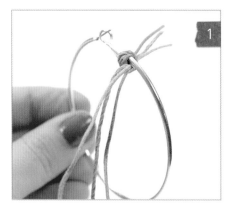

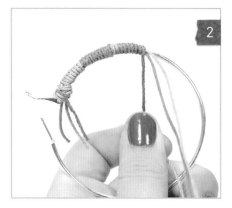

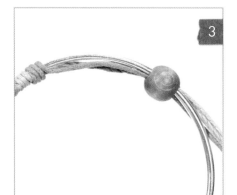

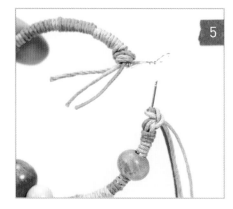

"I would rock these bold hoops with an equally bright and patterned dress to really create a stand-out ensemble!"

**—CHRISTINE CAMERON,
PERSONAL STYLIST
AND FASHION BLOGGER,
WWW.MYSTYLEPILL.COM**

GOLD STATEMENT NECKLACE

Inspired by Olivia Palermo

THE LOOK

SKILL LEVEL:

✂ ✂ ✂ ✂

WHAT YOU NEED:

10 straws
Scissors
Toothpicks
Piece of cardboard
Gold spray paint
Extra-long shoestrings,
  or black nylon cord
6 gold hex nuts

OLIVIA PALERMO'S LAYERED OUTFITS, love of patterns, and jewelry collaborations have many looking to her for fashion cues. Her gold choker was the inspiration for this necklace made from the most unassuming materials: straws and shoestring.

1. Cut 30 pieces of straw, each 1" (2.5cm) long.

2. Pierce 30 toothpicks through the cardboard, and put a piece of straw on each toothpick.

3. Cover the straws with a light coat of spray paint. Let dry and cover with a second coat. Repeat until straws are evenly covered.

4. When dry, take the first piece of straw and thread one shoestring through the left side, and a second shoestring through the right side. Take a second piece of straw and repeat.

5. Continue this cross-threading pattern with all the straw pieces.

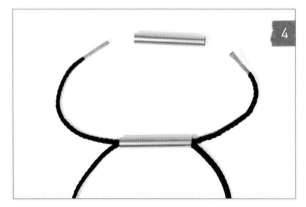

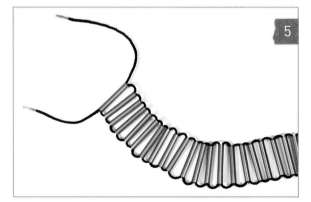

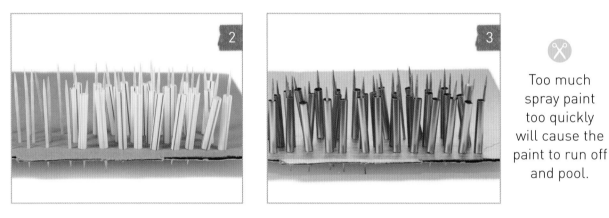

Too much spray paint too quickly will cause the paint to run off and pool.

6. Create the U shape by pulling on the bottom shoestring and adjust the straws to make a curve that will lie around your neck.

7. Knot the strings where the straws end, then thread 3 hex nuts onto the strings. Tie another knot. Repeat on the other side.

8. Snip off one piece of rope. Reinforce the knot with a dab of superglue.

9. To create an adjustable necklace, double-knot the right rope to the left side, and the left rope to the right side. Slide knots to adjust length.

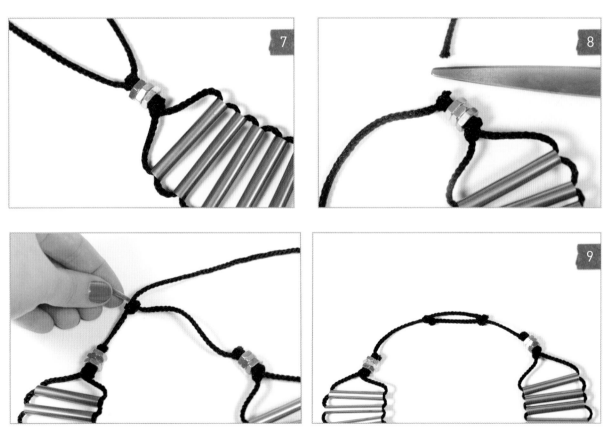

Love the mixed metal trend? Spray-paint half the straws gold and half silver. Wear your finished necklace with gold and silver bangle bracelets.

"I look **everywhere** for inspiration, anything that catches my eye. I always have my camera, and take pictures so I can capture the moments that **inspire** me."

—OLIVIA PALERMO

SAFETY PIN NECKLACE AND ANKLE-STRAP HEELS

Inspired by Jessica Alba

THE LOOK

JESSICA ALBA EMBODIES CHIC from head to toe in this sleek outfit. Safety pins and ribbon can be transformed into a similar statement necklace and ankle-strap heels. Just add a little black dress to complete the look!

SAFETY PIN NECKLACE

SKILL LEVEL:

✂ ✂ ✂ ✂

WHAT YOU NEED:

3 x 5" (7.5cm x 12.5cm) piece of black leather
Silver marker or chalk
Gold and silver safety pins (all the same size)
Scissors
Multipurpose glue
1"- (2.5cm-) wide black ribbon, cut into two 6" (15cm) lengths
1 Velcro square

MAKE IT!

1. Using a marker or chalk, draw a U on the black piece of leather. Make the U as thick as the width of your safety pins.

2. Cut out the U.

3. Slide safety pins onto the U.

4. Alternate between ten gold and ten silver safety pins until all but 1" (2.5cm) on each side of the U is covered.

5. Using multipurpose glue, adhere the remaining inch of leather to one 6" (15cm) piece of ribbon. Glue the second piece of ribbon to the other side of the leather. Let dry for 1 hour.

6. Stick the top of the Velcro square to one end of the ribbon, and the bottom of the Velcro square to the other end of the ribbon.

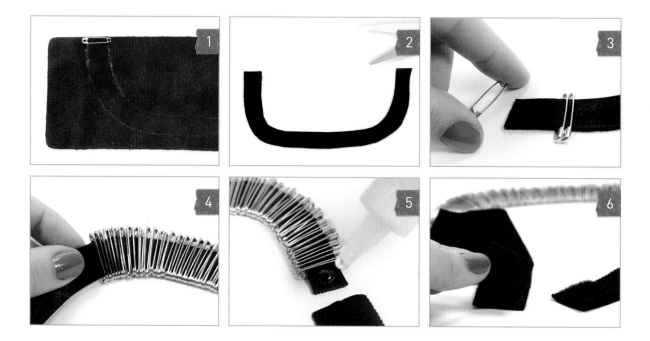

ANKLE-STRAP HEELS

WHAT YOU NEED:

1"- (2.5cm-) wide black ribbon in desired length
Scissors
Multipurpose glue
1 Velcro square
Pair of black pumps

MAKE IT!

1. To measure the length of ribbon needed, wrap it around your ankle, then add 2" (5cm) and cut. Cut a second piece the same length.

2. Fold one end of the ribbon over ½" (13mm) and glue it down.

3. Press down for a minute to let dry, then repeat on the other end.

4. Stick the top of the Velcro square onto the inside edge of the ribbon. Then stick the bottom square to the opposite ribbon edge on the outside.

5. Cut a 4"- (10cm-) piece of ribbon. Fold in half, forming a loop around the first piece of ribbon, and glue the bottom inch (2.5cm) of the two ends together. Let dry.

6. Glue the bottom inch (2.5cm) of the ribbon loop to the inside back of your shoe. Repeat on the second shoe and let dry.

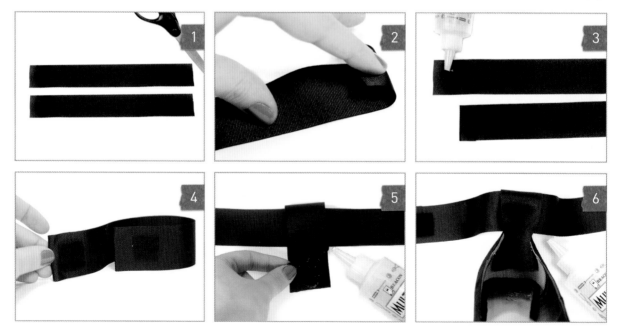

"Call me modest, but I have a rule; the higher the heel, the lower the hemline. To show off the ankle straps, I'd wear these with slightly cropped skinny jeans or with a tunic over leggings."

—ALISON DAHL, DESIGNER AND CREATIVE DIRECTOR OF WWW.BURDASTYLE.COM

These two projects complement each other perfectly, but they don't need to be worn together. The safety pin necklace is one of my daily go-to DIY pieces; I wear it with everything! Letting it peek out under a slouchy white shirt is one of my favorite ways.

CHOPSTICK DRESS
Inspired by Heidi Klum

THE LOOK
Designed with **Rachel Roy**

SKILL LEVEL:

✗ ✗ ✗ ✗

WHAT YOU NEED:

Dress
1 Plastic garbage bag
Bleach
Cookie sheet
Chopsticks

"To get a similar look to Heidi's, you need a solid-colored piece of clothing, bleach, and chopsticks. Dip a chopstick into the bleach and touch it to the fabric, but only for a second so you don't damage the fabric. Make your own personal print."

—RACHEL ROY, DESIGNER

THE PATTERN PLAY on Heidi Klum's dress is as striking as the super-model and *Project Runway* host herself. Rachel Roy, the designer of Heidi's dress, as well as dresses worn by Michelle Obama, Gwyneth Paltrow, and Halle Berry, lets us in on how to get the look!

1. Lay your dress flat, then line the inside with a garbage bag, separating the front from the back of the dress. This will prevent bleach from soaking though the garment.

2. Pour a thin layer of bleach onto the cookie sheet. Coat one chopstick with bleach.

3. Lightly touch the coated chopstick to the dress.

4. Continue to dip the chopstick in bleach and onto the dress, first the front and then the back. Cover the fabric with random lines to create the desired pattern.

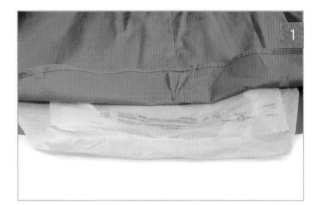

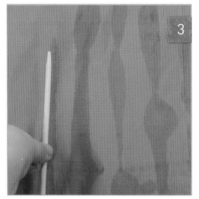

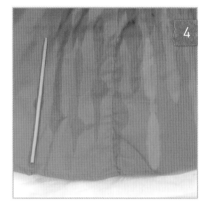

5. Let dry overnight. Bleached areas may take a few hours to lighten. Machine wash separately the first time.

Fabrics will bleach differently. Test on a cotton or secondhand store dress to find the material that will yield the best results, and perfect your technique.

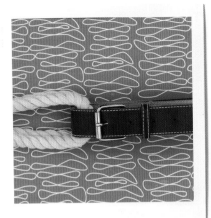

TWO

RIGHT FROM THE RUNWAY

The runway is the place I most often turn to when seeking inspiration for my next project. Each season, designers present us with a wealth of looks, providing endless ideas to spark a new DIY project. Since **Fashion Week** happens months before these new styles hit stores, it is an advance look at trends to come. If polka dots pop up on three runways, I guarantee spots will show up in stores across the country. By re-creating what the models are sporting, you can be **ahead of the trend**, and wear a custom version of what your friends will be scouring the stores for later.

Focus on a look, and think about how you can fashion it: copper piping becomes a Cynthia Rowley–inspired necklace (page 64), your everyday belt combined with rope makes a Michael Kors–esque waist cincher (page 50), and some fabric paint transforms a white dress into a **colorful head turner** inspired by my favorite designer, Marc Jacobs (page 54). On the runway is where fashion shines, so get inspired and make it your own!

ROPE BELT

Inspired by Michael Kors

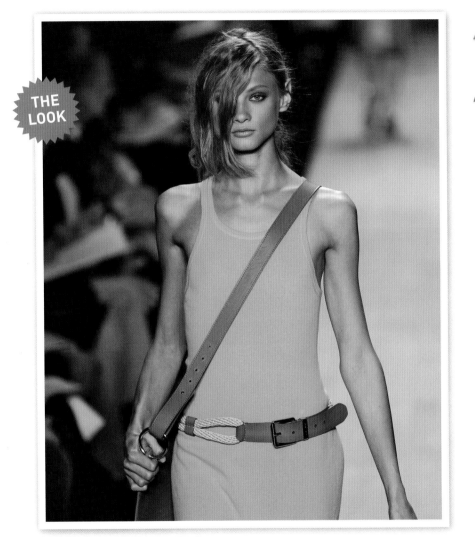

THE LOOK

SKILL LEVEL:

✂ ✂ ✂ ✂

WHAT YOU NEED:

Small piece of tan suede
Scissors
Rope
Superglue
Belt

GIVE AN EVERYDAY BELT a nautical spin by adding rope, à la Michael Kors's runway look. Wear it with a bright maxidress or a high-waisted sailor pant to add interest to your waistline.

1. Cut a 2 x 3" (5cm x 7.5cm) piece of suede.

2. Measure the rope by wrapping it around your waist once and then cut.

3. Make a figure eight by bringing both ends of the rope to its center, and place the suede under the area where the rope ends meet.

4. Superglue the two rope ends together. Fold one side of the suede over the rope and glue.

5. Fold over the other side of the suede and glue it closed. Let dry.

6. Slide the two end loops of the rope onto the belt.

7. Buckle the belt, and pull the back of the belt flat with the front. Unbuckle to wear.

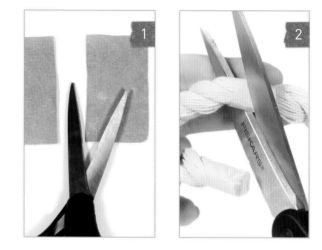

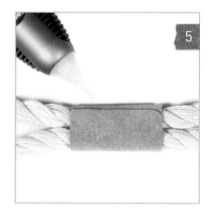

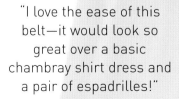
"I love the ease of this belt—it would look so great over a basic chambray shirt dress and a pair of espadrilles!"

—JESSICA QUIRK,
AUTHOR OF *WHAT I WORE*,
WWW.WHATIWORE.TUMBLR.COM

BRIGHT STRIPED DRESS AND MULTICOLORED BANGLES

Inspired by Marc Jacobs

THE LOOK

MARC JACOBS IS A CONSTANT SOURCE of inspiration, with his seemingly endless parade of brilliant ideas marching down the runway each season. This colorful creation was an immediate eye-catcher, inspiring a brightly striped dress and colorful bangles to match.

BRIGHT STRIPED DRESS

✂ ✂ ✂ ✂

WHAT YOU NEED:

White dress
Large plastic
  garbage bag
Masking tape
Fabric paint in four colors
Foam paintbrush

MAKE IT!

1. Lay the dress flat, lining the inside with a garbage bag to prevent paint from soaking through to the back side of the dress. Working from the bottom, lay down four strips of masking tape, 1½" (3.8cm) apart. The space in between the tape will create the stripes.

2. Using the foam brush, paint the bottom stripe.

3. Working your way up, paint each area between the masking tape a different color (wash the brush between each paint color change). Let paint dry for 12 hours.

4. Repeat steps 1-3 on the other side of the dress, making sure to line up the color stripes in the front and back. Let paint dry and remove the masking tape.

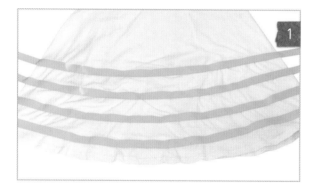

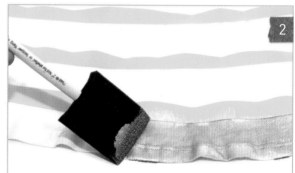

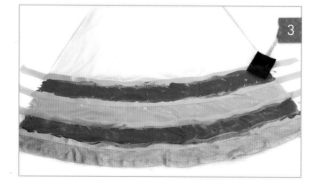

BUY CHAINS

PAINT FABRIC

PATCH JEANS

HOT GLUE GUN

BUY GLITTER

SAFETY PINS

SEW SEQUINS

STUD COLLAR

BRAID LEATHER

SEW BUTTON

JEWELED BELT

PATTERN

PAINT

NEEDLE + THREAD

DYE

TISSUE PAPER

FABRIC

TRIM

TAPE

HOT GLUE GUN

BEADS

SCISSORS

GLITTER SHOES

I absolutely adore Marc Jacobs's color combination, but if you think it is color overload, try muted tones, or stick to one color stripe.

MULTICOLORED BANGLES

SKILL LEVEL:

WHAT YOU NEED:

Raffia in bright colors (ribbon will also work)
Craft rings or plain bracelets

MAKE IT!

1. Double-knot the raffia on the craft ring, leaving a few inches (approx. 5cm) of excess raffia on one side and the rest of the raffia on the other.

2. Next, tie a single knot of raffia around the ring and pull it tight so it sits close to the double knot.

3. Continue making single knots and then pulling tight, working your way around the ring.

4. When the entire ring is covered, double-knot the excess raffia you left at the beginning to the end of the raffia, and cut off any excess.

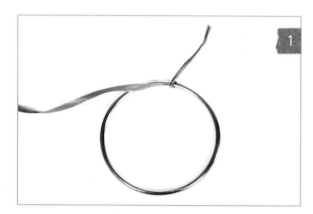

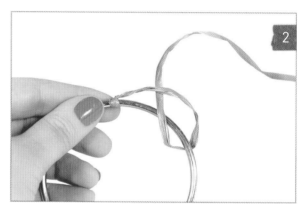

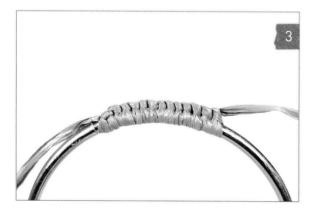

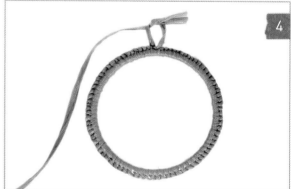

"These bracelets are so colorful and fun, I would mix and match them with a chunky watch and other gold accessories to make a pretty arrangement of bangles on my wrist."

—CHRISTINE CAMERON, PERSONAL STYLIST AND FASHION BLOGGER, WWW.MYSTYLEPILL.COM

SHEER SCARF SHIRT

Inspired by Jenni Packham

THE LOOK

SKILL LEVEL:

✗ ✗ ✗ ✗

WHAT YOU NEED:

Large square scarf
Piece of nonstretch
  fabric (same size or
  larger than the scarf)
Scissors
Lighter
Needle and thread

REFASHION A GREAT SCARF into a breezy top. Use neglected scarves from your closet, or check your local Goodwill for gorgeous prints and patterns costing just a couple of dollars.

1. Lay the fabric flat, then lay the scarf on top. Cut the fabric to the same size as the scarf.

2. To prevent the fabric from fraying, quickly wave a lighter along the edges of all four sides of the fabric.

3. With wrong sides facing, lay the fabric and scarf flat, squaring the edges.

4. Using a simple whip-stitch, hand-sew the top edge, leaving a 6" (15cm) space in the middle for your head. On each side, starting at the bottom hem, stitch up 3" (7.5cm), to create armholes.

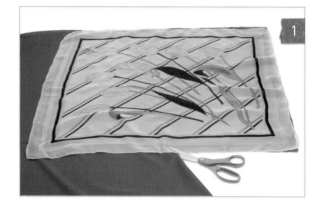

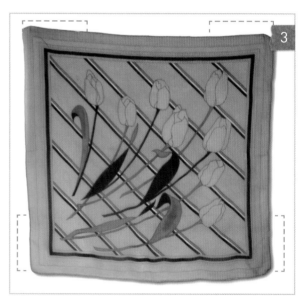

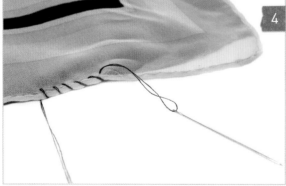

Depending on the
sheerness of your
scarf, wear your
new top with a nude,
white, or matching
colored tank. Try
tucking in your scarf
shirt, or wear it
untucked and belted.

DOUBLE PIPE NECKLACE
Inspired by Cynthia Rowley

THE LOOK

✗ ✗ ✗ ✗

WHAT YOU NEED:

At least 6" (15cm) of ¼"-
(6mm-) copper tubing
Mini tubing cutter
2 lobster clasps
4 spring ends
Rope (thin enough to fit
through piping)
Spray paint in two colors

WHEN RE-CREATING METAL JEWELRY like Cynthia Rowley's necklace, hardware stores are a DIYer's best friend. A few coats of spray paint transform copper piping, hex nuts, and rope into a striking accessory that can be doubled up or worn alone.

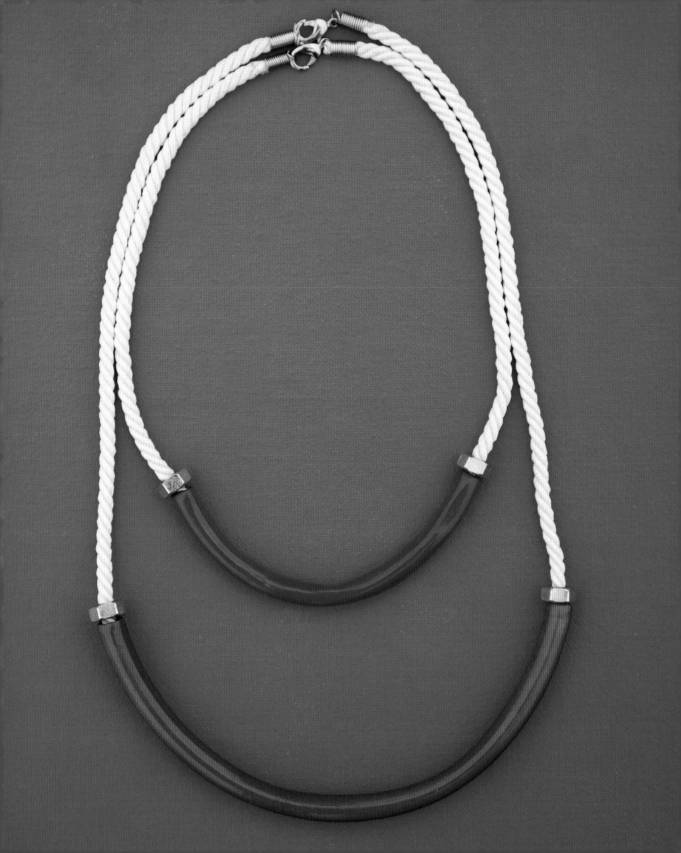

1. Measure 6" (15cm) of copper tubing, and using the cutter, tighten its clamp around the tubing.

2. Rotate cutter around the tubing, tightening the clamp with each rotation until the copper tubing is cut.

3. Repeat with second piece of tubing, and bend both pieces to lay as desired.

4. Spray-paint each piece a different color (in a well-ventilated area), and let dry overnight.

5. Thread rope through piping.

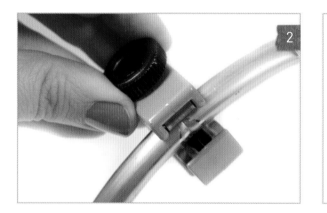

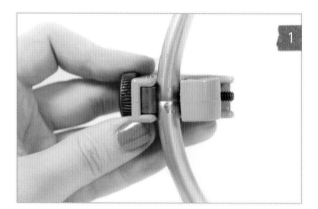

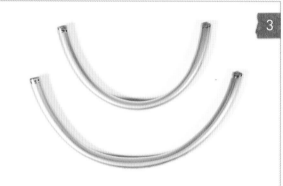

6. String a hex nut on each side.

7. Twist a spring end onto each rope end. Attach the coil of one spring end to the lobster claw, then attach the clasp to the opposite side to close.

8. Repeat with second necklace, using a longer length of string.

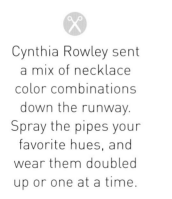

Cynthia Rowley sent a mix of necklace color combinations down the runway. Spray the pipes your favorite hues, and wear them doubled up or one at a time.

"One of the things we love most about **jewelry** is its ability to completely revamp whatever is in your closet, but at a fraction of the cost of overhauling your wardrobe. We are huge proponents of mixing high and low pieces and of **layering** on the baubles. Layering pieces in an innovative way, and infusing some homemade accessories is a great way to make sure your style is a unique expression of you."

—AMY JAIN & DANIELLA YACOBOVSKY,
CO-FOUNDERS OF BAUBLEBAR JEWELRY, WWW.BAUBLEBAR.COM

"These necklaces are clearly statement pieces and should be worn against a simple top or dress so that they remain the focus of the overall ensemble. They would also look great paired with a plain denim button-down or a white V-neck."

—CHRISTINE CAMERON, PERSONAL STYLIST AND FASHION BLOGGER, WWW.MYSTYLEPILL.COM

SILVER BAUBLE NECKLACE
Inspired by Milly

THE LOOK

SKILL LEVEL:

✗ ✗ ✗ ✗

WHAT YOU NEED:

1 yd (91cm) 20-gauge wire
Diagonal pliers
40 large silver beads
10 clear vase gems
  (found in the floral
  department of any
  craft store)
2' (61cm) yellow ribbon

ALL IT TAKES TO MAKE YOUR FAVORITE DRESS a knockout is a statement necklace. Milly did just that, creating a stunner that can transition from work to a night out, and from a printed sundress to your basic LBD. Metallic beads and gems meld together harmoniously to create an accessory worth talking about.

1. Cut 3 pieces of wire, each 12" (30.5cm) long, using the diagonal pliers. String beads onto the wire, alternating between silver beads and gems, leaving 4" (10cm) of wire on each end. Create the bead/gem pattern you desire.

2. After you string all three wires, lay them down short to long. (Play around and make adjustments, so the beads and gems are arranged to your liking.)

3. Twist the ends of the three wires together and string four additional beads on each end.

4. Finish by making a loop with the wire. Beginning at the base of the loop, wrap the excess ends tightly around the wire.

5. Cut the ribbon in half and tie a piece to each wire loop.

"Reinvent your jewelry by layering! You can achieve a great look by combining different chains, stones, and charms. Don't be afraid to mix your gold and silver jewelry together—just remember to have fun and know that it is totally easy to do it yourself!"

—ROBYN RHODES, JEWELRY DESIGNER

Personalize this project by using multicolored beads or change the ribbon color.

PETAL BIB NECKLACE

Inspired by Erin Fetherston

THE LOOK

SKILL LEVEL:

✄ ✄ ✄ ✄

WHAT YOU NEED:

1 yd (91cm) cream chiffon
2 x 20" (5cm x 51cm)
  length of cream tulle
Scissors
Foam visor (remove
  the coil connecting
  the two ends)
Needle and thread
2"- (5cm-) wide cream
  ribbon

ADD A TOUCH OF THE ETHEREAL to your wardrobe with a petal neckpiece inspired by Erin Fetherston. Wear this airy item with a light and loose frock, or create a striking contrast by pairing it with a bright, structured dress.

1. Cut forty 1½" (3.8cm) circles from the cream chiffon, and ten 2" (5cm) squares from the cream tulle.

2. Starting with the chiffon, fold each side of the circle to meet in the middle, creating a cone-shape petal.

3. With the needle and thread, attach the end point of the petal to the foam visor with a few stitches.

4. Repeat steps 1–3, covering the top and bottom edges of the visor first, then filling in the center.

5. Next, take a tulle square and fold it into an accordion pattern, then fold it in half.

Kids' foam visors, found at Hobby Lobby, are perfect for making bib necklaces.

6. Stitch the folded end of the tulle to the visor. Repeat stitching tulle to visor, filling in gaps between petals.

7. Cut two pieces of ribbon 12" (30.5cm) long and sew one to each end of the visor.

8. Tie ribbon around your neck.

"This was by far one of my favorite DIY pieces! This floral bib has such a great texture and feel to it. I love the pale cream color and would wear this over a bold-colored top, a pair of skinny jeans, and some sky-high heels. I love how this necklace can instantly glam up a simple T and jeans look."

—KIM PESCH, FASHION BLOGGER, WWW.EATSLEEPWEAR.COM

"I think it's important to collect **inspiration** as you go. Create a file where you keep **pictures** of things you like; then you have something to refer to when you actually get into DIY time."

—ERIN FETHERSTON, FASHION DESIGNER

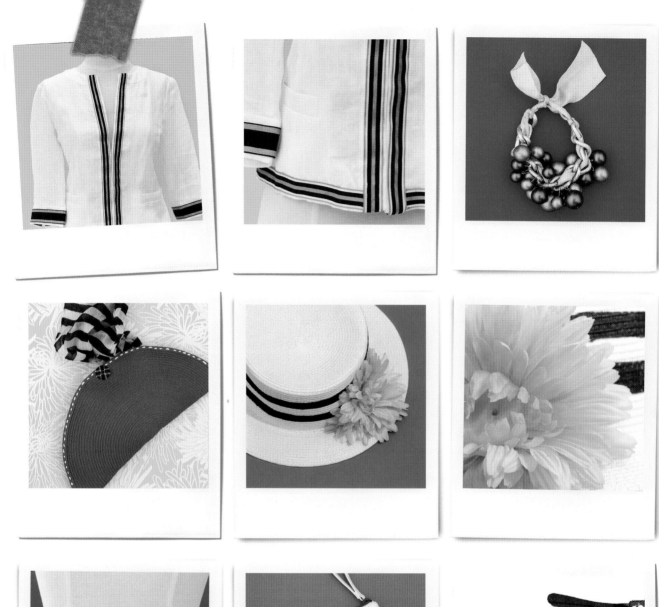

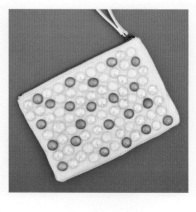

THREE

A TOUCH OF CLASSIC

Coco Chanel's designs are as fashionable now as they were in the 1920s, Elizabeth Taylor's bombshell style continues to captivate, and touches of **nautical whimsy** find their way onto the runway every season. Iconic beauties are often remembered for the way they dressed, certain designs will never look outdated, and some trends will never go out of style. When searching for a project that will stylistically stand **the test of time**, what better place to look than to the classics? Take a vintage style you like and update it by experimenting with **unusual materials**. Turn a place mat into a clutch inspired by a Bridgette Bardot ensemble (page 92) or bling out a belt with **glass vase beads** from the floral department (page 102). Referencing looks from decades past that continue to be worn today is a foolproof way to always be on trend.

RIBBON-LINED JACKET

Inspired by Coco Chanel

THE LOOK

✗ ✗ ✗ ✗

WHAT YOU NEED:

White nonstretch jacket
4–5 yd (3.5–4.5m) striped
  ribbon
Fabric glue
Small paintbrush

CHANEL EMBODIES ALL THINGS FASHION, so why not look to Coco herself for inspiration? Her lined hems have been a brand staple through-out the years. All you need is a little ribbon to re-create the timeless tech-nique and reinvent a casual linen jacket.

1. With the jacket laid flat, measure along the edges, including both cuffs, each side of the jacket opening, and the entire circumference of the bottom edge. After tracing each area, cut the ribbon for each edge, leaving 1" (2.5cm) of excess at each end of ribbon length.

2. Working from bottom to top, start by gluing the vertical strips of ribbon to the jacket, leaving 1" (2.5cm) of overhang on the bottom. Use the paintbrush to spread the glue, covering the entire width of the ribbon.

3. Fold the excess inch (2.5cm) of ribbon over and glue to the inside of the jacket on the top and bottom.

Use one size of ribbon for a uniform look, or experiment with different widths or styles of stripe as I did here.

4. Next, glue the ribbon to the bottom edge by tucking the start of the ribbon under the vertical strip on the right. Glue the ribbon around the circumference of the jacket and then tuck the end under the vertical strip on the left.

5. Dab glue where the ribbons intersect to secure.

6. Finish the look by lining the cuffs. If sleeves have a slit, fold the ribbon and glue it to the inside lining. If not, glue the ribbon to itself.

7. Let dry for 24 hours.

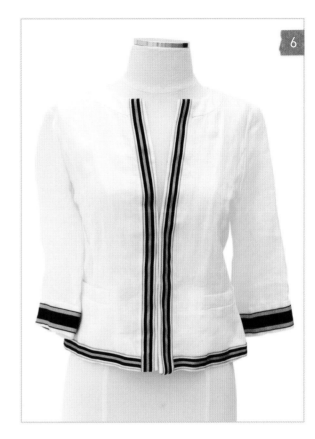

USE THE EXTRAS: RIBBON BELT

Make a matching belt with extra ribbon!

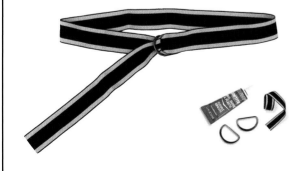

SKILL LEVEL:

✂ ✂ ✂ ✂

WHAT YOU NEED:

2 D-rings
Ribbon (to your measurements)
Fabric glue

MAKE IT!

1. Measure ribbon by wrapping it around your waist, then add 5" (12.5cm).

2. Thread 2" (5cm) of ribbon through both D-rings, then glue the ribbon to itself.

3. Let dry for 24 hours.

"I love the idea of people making or embellishing their own clothing. I think it's a great way for people to get inspired and personalize their look. **Coco Chanel** professed that 'true beauty is uniqueness'; therefore, when you look like other people, you are relinquishing your own beauty. I encourage my girls and my customers to **be unique**, to have a distinct point of view and share it with the world."

—RACHEL ROY, DESIGNER

"I'd go Old Hollywood with this jacket and pair it with some cropped black pants and flats!"

**—JESSICA QUIRK,
AUTHOR OF** *WHAT I WORE*,
WWW.WHATIWORE.TUMBLR.COM

Pair this jacket with a pencil skirt for a sleek look, or put a polished spin on jeans and a T-shirt.

PEARL BEADED BRACELET

Inspired by Grace Kelly

THE LOOK

WHAT YOU NEED:

Round beads in assorted
  sizes and colors
Silver headpins
6" (15cm) silver chain
Needle-nose pliers
12" (30.5cm) cream-
  colored ribbon

CREATE A CLASSIC BRACELET fit not only for a movie star, but for a princess. Mimic the look of Grace Kelly's gorgeous baubles and you are sure to make a piece that will withstand the test of time.

1. Thread a bead onto a headpin.

2. Using your pliers, loop the headpin around a link on the chain, and then wrap the end tightly around the wire, attaching the bead securely to the chain.

3. Repeat steps 1-2 until the middle of the chain is covered.

4. Tie the ribbon to one end of the chain.

5. Thread the ribbon though the links of the chain and knot on the opposite side.

6. Tie onto your wrist.

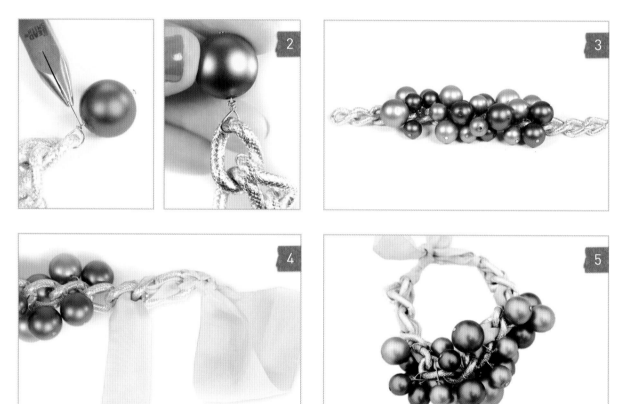

"I love wearing bold bracelets with basic dresses and jeans alike!"

—JESSICA QUIRK,
AUTHOR OF *WHAT I WORE*,
WWW.WHATIWORE.TUMBLR.COM

NAUTICAL BAG

Inspired by Brigitte Bardot

THE LOOK

SKILL LEVEL:

✄ ✄ ✄ ✄

WHAT YOU NEED:

Round red rattan
    place mat
1 yd (91cm) thin white
    ribbon
Tapestry needle
Magnetic purse clasps
Needle-nose pliers
Nautical pin

ICONIC BOMBSHELL BRIGITTE BARDOT epitomized what the French call *"je ne sais quois,"* always appearing perfectly pulled together. Capture this look with a clutch that is truly St. Tropez chic!

1. Fold the place mat in half. Starting at one end, stitch the two sides together, using a simple running stitch with the tapestry needle and the ribbon.

2. Once you are a third of the way around, stitch only the front side of the place mat, creating the opening for your clutch.

3. When you have stitched two-thirds of the way around the mat, resume stitching the front and back together until you reach the end.

4. Knot the ribbon at both ends and cut off the excess.

5. Next, position the purse clasps in the middle of the clutch opening, and push the prongs though the place mat.

6. Using the needle-nose pliers, bend the metal prongs down to secure the clasps on the front and back of your clutch.

7. Cover the clasp with a nautical pin. Or use an earring!

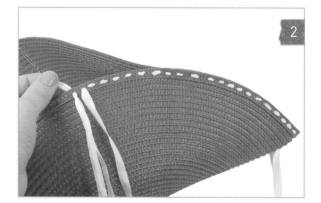

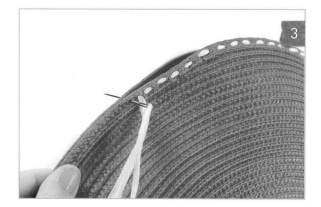

> "Just go for what you like, regardless of how something is meant to be worn or used. Don't be afraid to test the waters and do something completely random— if you like it, then rock it."

—KIRSTEN NUNEZ, DIY BLOGGER, WWW.STUDS-AND-PEARLS.COM

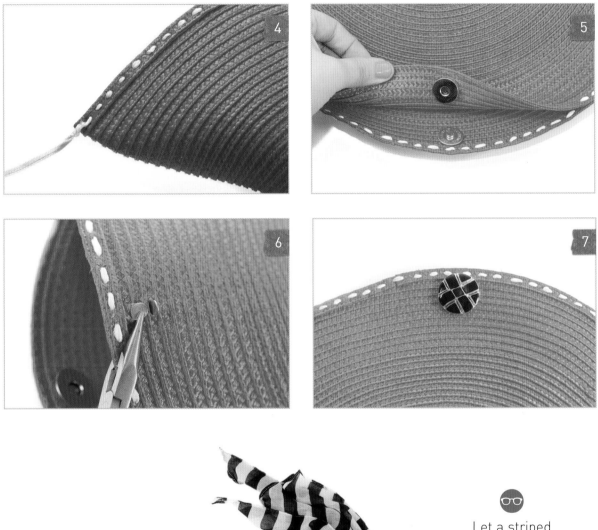

Let a striped scarf hang from the edge of your clutch to complete the look.

"Look at retro fashion photography and **old movie stills** for inspiration, because everything comes back, but not in the same way. It gives you a place not to copy but to **adapt.**"

—HAL RUBENSTEIN, FASHION DIRECTOR FOR *INSTYLE* MAGAZINE

STRIPED HAT

Inspired by Audrey Hepburn

THE LOOK

✂ ✂ ✂ ✂

WHAT YOU NEED:

White hat
Masking tape
Black acrylic paint
Paintbrush
Fabric flower
Earring with post
  and back

AUDREY HEPBURN IS THE ULTIMATE CLASSIC ICON, embodying beauty, style, and grace. Her Holly Golightly character from *Breakfast at Tiffany's* effortlessly throws on a hat and achieves instant chic in one of my favorite film scenes. I was inspired by Audrey's striped topper, which strikes the perfect balance between casual and dressy.

1. Place three evenly spaced strips of masking tape around the top part of the hat.

2. Using the paint-brush, cover the space in between the tape with black acrylic paint.

3. Let paint dry for 2 hours, and then peel off the tape to reveal your stripes.

4. Add a little color to your hat by removing the stem and the middle part of a fabric flower and attaching it to the hat, using an earring to pin the flower through the center.

"Nothing could be a better nod to old-world charm than a wide-brimmed hat with a flower. So polished, and very Park Avenue!"

—KIM PESCH, FASHION BLOGGER, WWW.EATSLEEPWEAR.COM

BEJEWELED BELT

Inspired by Elizabeth Taylor

THE LOOK

SKILL LEVEL:

✂ ✂ ✂ ✂

WHAT YOU NEED:

2 yd (1.8m) silver ribbon
Scissors
Multipurpose glue
Flat vase gems (found in the floral department of any craft store)

NO ONE DID GLAMOUR BETTER than Elizabeth Taylor. She was never afraid to shine, and her white dress and matching clutch is anything but basic. Add a little Elizabeth in your life by bedazzling a belt and bag with gems almost as precious.

1. Cut a piece of silver ribbon long enough to wrap around your waist twice.

2. Start gluing gems to the middle of the ribbon using multipurpose glue.

3. Glue gems close together, and cover the middle 10" (25.5cm) of the ribbon.

4. Let dry for 24 hours. Tie around your waist, letting the bow hang in the back.

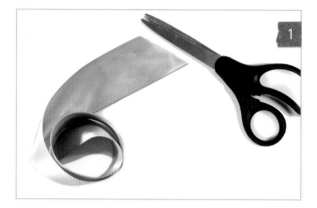

♀ USE THE EXTRAS:
BEJEWELED CLUTCH

Grab your glue and add gems to a plain purse.

"I love the sculptural quality to these pebbled pieces. I would wear this belt to cinch a flowy dress and give my body some shape. I also love how neutral the color palette is in the clutch. It would go great with either a classic LBD for a dinner date, or with a bright shift dress for cocktails with the girls."

—KIM PESCH, FASHION BLOGGER, WWW.EATSLEEPWEAR.COM

FEATHER HEADBAND

THE LOOK
Designed with
Gretchen Jones

SKILL LEVEL:

✂ ✂ ✂ ✂

WHAT YOU NEED:

Plastic headband
Snakeskin or metallic
 leather
Sharpie
Scissors
Glue gun
Feathers
Flat studs

FROM FLAPPERS IN THE ROARING '20S to free spirits in the '60s to today, designers have repeatedly found ways to use feathers in fashion. Designer and *Project Runway* Season 8 winner Gretchen Jones modernized this evergreen trend, when she stopped by my apartment to show me how to make a feather headband.

Gretchen hot-glued feathers facing up and down to create a feather "bow." She wrapped leather around the center and topped it off with a stud.

1. Cut a thin strip of leather a little thicker than the width of the headband.

2. Measure the length by marking the leather at one tip of the headband, then roll the headband along the leather and mark at the opposite tip.

3. Cut a curved edge where you made each mark.

4. Using a glue gun, start at one end of the headband and cover it with hot glue a few inches at a time, adhering the leather strip to the headband.

5. Dab a bit of glue approximately 4" (10cm) from one end of the headband, and then place three stacked feathers in the dab of glue, quills facing toward the end of the headband.

6. Let dry for 10 seconds, and then cut off excess feather. I added a blue feather after this step for a splash of color!

7. Cover feather ends by wrapping a thin piece of leather around both the feather ends and the headband. Glue the leather end to itself to secure in place.

8. Add some studs by gluing them into place on the leather.

"I think the beauty of this project is you can really wear it with anything, depending on how you adorn yours. It looks great with just jeans and a T for a casual cool-girl effect, and also looks pretty and sophisticated alongside dresses. *And*, depending on what colors you use, they are perfect accessories for weddings or other fancy affairs!"

—GRETCHEN JONES

6 TIPS FOR
THROWING A DIY PARTY

One of my favorite things about DIY is that it is contagious. Now instead of immediately buying a new piece, my friends ask if we can get together to make their latest fashion obsession.

1 Pick a project that works for **every skill level**. Headbands and friendship bracelets can range from simple to super intricate.

2 Try out a few of the projects or techniques ahead of time, so you can **teach** your guests rather than get bogged down trying to figure out how to make something work.

3 Get extra supplies from your local **dollar store**, so your guests will not have to wait in line for glue or scissors.

4 Stop by the fabric store to see if they have leftover trimming **scraps** you can take off their hands.

5 **Print out instructions** for a few projects, so your friends can refer to their "cheat sheet" while working.

6 Serve **simple snacks**, so you can spend your time crafting instead of running to the kitchen.

FOUR

UPDATE YOUR BASICS

A button-down shirt, a pair of jeans, and a plain tank top are **wardrobe staples** that everyone has in the closet. Often we find ourselves with multiples of these items. Instead of tossing your extras, **refashion these pieces** with some studs, a bright ribbon, or a playful pattern. With a few simple steps, you can transform these items into wearables that are anything but basic. Unexpected materials, like brackets from your hardware store, give a plain clutch a structured metallic makeover (page 134). Or return to a childhood favorite and use puffy paint to give your black flats a **faux-stud effect** (page 138). Take an everyday item and make it into a statement piece with simple embellishments. Pins, trimmings, and rhinestones are just a few ways to reinvigorate your LBD into an ensemble worth talking about.

RIBBON TANK

Frame your face by weaving ribbon around the neckline of a tank top.

SKILL LEVEL:

WHAT YOU NEED:

Tank top
Pencil
Scissors
Ribbon

Color choices are endless! Also try different ribbon widths and other materials to create a look you love.

1. Turn your tank top inside out. With a pencil, draw markings around the neckline, alternating between a ½" (13mm) space and 1½" (3.8cm) space.

2. Using scissors, make a snip at each mark no wider then the width of the ribbon.

3. Turn your tank top right side out. Thread the ribbon through the holes, so the ribbon shows on the outside of the tank top in the larger gaps.

4. Tie a bow where the two ends of ribbon meet. Leave the tails long, or cut to make a more tidy bow.

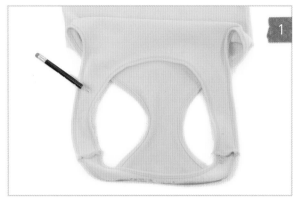

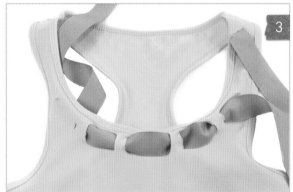

To prevent any chance of fraying, dab fabric glue where you've snipped.

"I love when people **customize** things in their wardrobe. A fun way to start is by embellishing a simple T-shirt. You can use **anything** from fabric scraps to ribbon or beads to create special custom details."

—ERIN FETHERSTON, FASHION DESIGNER

5 QUICK IDEAS TO
TRANSFORM A T-SHIRT

1 **Tie-dye is back**, but in an updated way. For a more sophisticated effect, stick with one color and a basic pattern. Try wrapping thick rubber bands around the top, middle, and bottom areas of your shirt, and then dye it. This will create a striped look after the dye sets.

2 To amp up the va-va-voom, **cut a hole** in the back of a shirt, then use fabric glue to add a piece of lace or sheer fabric to the inside of the shirt to create an interesting peek-a-boo.

3 To turn your basic white T preppy, sew 3-5 **nautical buttons** down the front. Or use pearl buttons on the front of a black T-shirt for a more classic look.

4 Jazz up your casual T-shirt by hand-stitching **embellished trim** around the neckline or sleeves. Make sure to use trims made with stretch or elastic thread so you can still easily pull your shirt off and on.

5 Give your T-shirt an instant **tribal look**. Cut different size triangles out of paper. Then turn your T-shirt inside out and place the triangles around the neck of your T-shirt in an interesting pattern. When you like the placement, use a pencil to trace around each shape and then cut out.

METALLIC LACE JEAN MINI

Combining denim and lace creates a perfect balance between tough and delicate. Give your jean skirt a metallic touch using a lace place mat to create the pattern.

SKILL LEVEL:

✗ ✗ ✗ ✗

WHAT YOU NEED:

Jean skirt
Lace
Masking tape
Foam paintbrush
Fabric paint in silver
Iron

1. Lay the lace on the corner of the jean skirt, and then cut the lace to fit the area you want to paint. Secure it in place with masking tape.

2. Using the foam brush, paint the lace with silver fabric paint. Lightly dabbing the paint works best to keep it from seeping under the lace.

3. After covering the lace area, let it dry.

4. Peel off the lace to reveal the metallic pattern. Repeat on the opposite side or the back, as desired.

5. When paint is dry, turn the skirt inside out and iron it on medium heat to set the fabric paint.

Use a lace that has large holes so you can see the denim through the pattern. A lace place mat or table runner from your dollar store works great and is inexpensive!

Try this same technique on a pair of jeans or a denim jacket. Or change up the colors and use black paint on a pair of red jeans.

"I make a lot of my clothing, but reconstructing an already ready-to-wear garment is an **easy and affordable** way to breathe new life into something ordinary. Even the tiniest tweaks—adjusting a hemline, switching up the sleeves, adding a trim or a cutout—can **personalize** a garment and make it something unique."

—KEIKO GROVES, DESIGNER OF POSTLAPSARIA AND FASHION BLOGGER, WWW.KEIKOLYNN.COM

5 IDEAS TO
REFASHION YOUR JEANS

1 Use Rit dye to transform your basic blues into an **autumnal color** as the seasons change. Use a medium wash denim and let it soak in a bucket of deep green, burgundy, or burnt orange. Follow the instructions on the back of the dye.

2 Give your jeans a rocker edge by **studding** the pockets of your favorite well-worn pair. Using a seam ripper, detach one corner of your jeans pocket, and stud the inside.

3 Cut a slit on the bottom of each leg and stitch on a **zipper**. Use skinny jeans and wear zipped down, or open over a pair of boots.

4 Give your jeans luxe appeal by **painting a stripe** down the sides with gold or silver fabric paint. Tape off the area you want metallic, then paint inside the lines. Want something bolder? Use neon paint to really make a statement.

5 The perfect mix of trends—**lace, sheer, and wide-leg jeans**—is easy to achieve. Combine them by taking a pair of your straight-leg jeans, cut the side seam to just above your knee, and then sew in a triangular piece of lace. This will give the bottom of your jeans some volume, and the sheer lace will keep the look from getting bulky.

DESIGNER IDEA

Cut off the back pockets on a pair of jeans. Then hand-stitch one onto the front of a sweater, or add a fun detail to your winter scarf by sewing a pocket on each end.

—JOYCE AZRIA, CREATIVE DIRECTOR OF BCBGENERATION

STUDDED BUTTON-DOWN

Give your basic
button-down
shirt a studly
makeover.

SKILL LEVEL:

WHAT YOU NEED:

Collared button-down
  shirt
Pronged studs in
  assorted sizes and
  metal colors
Needle-nose pliers

1. Poke studs through the front of the shirt collar.

2. On the backside, use pliers to push down the prongs and secure the stud to the shirt.

3. Repeat, mixing different sizes and alternating gold and silver until the entire collar is covered.

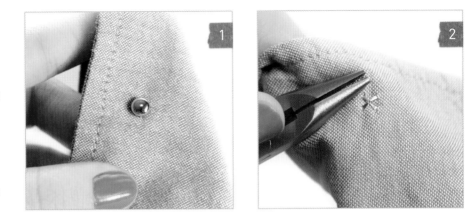

Skip a necklace and let the studded collar shine, or add an armful of bracelets to balance your heavy metal.

"When adding embellishment, place it by your best features, a part of your body you want to celebrate, like your neckline or hemline, because that is where you will bring my eye."

—HAL RUBENSTEIN, *INSTYLE* FASHION DIRECTOR

SPARKLE SKIRT

Feeling festive?
Stand apart
from the rest
with some
shimmer and
shine on your
skirt, topped
off with a bow.

SKILL LEVEL:

✗ ✗ ✗ ✗

WHAT YOU NEED:

Plain nonstretch skirt
2 yd (1.8m) ribbon,
   sequined or metallic
Fabric glue such
   as Liquid Stitch

1. Lay your skirt flat and place a piece of cardboard between the layers to prevent the glue from seeping through to the back.

2. Cut a piece of sequined ribbon the length of your skirt, leaving 1½" (3.8cm) of excess at the top and bottom. Apply glue to the back of the ribbon.

3. Place ribbon on the center of the skirt, then fold the excess over the top and bottom edges and glue to the inside.

4. Next, create the bow by cutting two pieces of sequined ribbon, one 6" (15cm) and the other 3" (7.5cm) long. Fold the ends of the longer piece toward the center, and glue at the middle.

5. Place the shorter piece underneath vertically, and then apply glue on both sides, folding toward the center.

6. Attach the bow to the top of your skirt with a good amount of glue. Let dry for 24 hours.

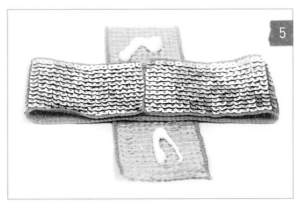

If you buy a heavy beaded trim, hand-stitch it on to ensure it stays in place.

"This skirt pops on its own, and it's so romantic and girly— I'd pair it with a frilly vintage camisole and flats."

—ALISON DAHL, DESIGNER AND CREATIVE DIRECTOR OF WWW.BURDASTYLE.COM

"When you **make something** yourself, it automatically becomes more 'you' than if you had bought a similar piece. The **satisfaction** you get from wearing something that you've made yourself is second to none."

—GENEVA VANDERZEIL, DIY BLOGGER, WWW.APAIR-ANDASPARE.BLOGSPOT.COM

CHECKERED SUNGLASSES

Up the cool factor on your sunglasses with a silver Sharpie and a steady hand.

SKILL LEVEL:

✗ ✗ ✗ ✗

WHAT YOU NEED:

Plastic sunglasses
Silver Sharpie

Enhance the effect by starting with colorful sunglasses as the base.

1. Using a silver metallic Sharpie, start at one end of your sunglasses and draw diagonal lines across the entire face of the glasses. Let dry for a few minutes.

2. Next, draw diagonal lines in the opposite direction to create a crosshatch pattern.

The markings are permanent, so practice on a piece of paper before taking the marker to your sunglasses!

"With trends moving so quickly, I think it is important to experiment with things in your own closet, find ways to style them a different way."

—CHRIS BENZ, FASHION DESIGNER

TIED ROPE NECKLACE

What's *knot* to love about this necklace?

SKILL LEVEL:

✗ ✗ ✗ ✗

WHAT YOU NEED:

1 yd (91cm) black rope
2 yd (1.8m) gold rope
Superglue
D-ring
Clasp

1. Cut the gold rope in half and arrange the three pieces of rope in an S shape, with the black rope in the middle.

2. Tuck the top rope end of the S under the bottom left curve.

3. Tuck the bottom rope end under the right curve.

4. Pull the rope tight, keeping the knot flat.

5. Dab superglue around the knot to keep it in place.

6. Tie one end of the three ropes in a knot around the flat end of the D-ring. Then knot the other end of the ropes around the clasp.

7. Cut off the excess rope and superglue the knot to hold in place.

"I make a fashion trend my own by always adding something **unexpected**—it could be black pants with an ostrich feather fascinator or a bright purple flower on a Burberry trench. **Fashion** is a state of mind and your style should be a direct reflection of your world view."

—KATHRYN FINNEY, AUTHOR AND FOUNDER, WWW.THEBUDGETFASHIONISTA.COM

HARDWARE CLUTCHES

Give your clutch a heavy-metal edge with supplies from your local hardware store.

WHAT YOU NEED:

Tablet or eReader case
  or clutch
Four 3" (7.5cm) flat iron
  corners
Safety hasp
Lock
Superglue

1. Cover the back of the iron corner with superglue.

2. Place the iron on the corner of your clutch and hold for 30 seconds. Repeat on all four corners.

3. Next, cover the back of your safety hasp with superglue.

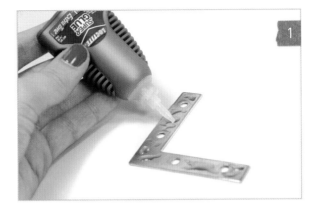

♀ THE EVENING ALTERNATIVE

For evening, use a small black clutch and add gold metal to the top two corners for a subtle, sophisticated look.

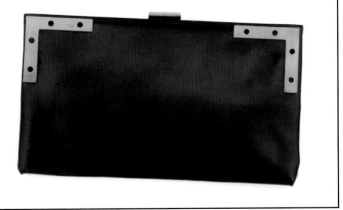

4. Place the safety hasp in the center of the flap on the clutch. Let dry for one hour.

5. Add lock!

Envelope-style eReader cases work perfectly because most lie flat and have square corners.

Juxtapose this structured clutch with a ruffled frock, or wear it with a fitted sheath dress for a streamlined look.

"We love the DIY movement, especially taking something old and worn out and making it new and your own. **What's not to love?** We definitely encourage everyone to try DIY. Sometimes, after growing up, we often forget what it felt like to be **creative** in our younger years. It brings back great memories and often helps relieve stress."

—M&J TRIMMINGS, WWW.MJTRIM.COM

SPIKED FLATS

Toughen up your flats with a Louboutin-like upgrade. People won't believe your "spikes" are made from puffy paint.

SKILL LEVEL:

✗ ✗ ✗ ✗

WHAT YOU NEED:

Black flats
Silver puffy paint

1. Starting at the front of the shoe, dab a spot of paint onto the top, pulling the nozzle directly up to create a point. As the paint dries, it turns from gray to a shiny metallic.

2. Repeat dabbing to create rows of "spikes" all along the sides of the shoe.

3. Let dry for 24 hours in an area where the shoes will not be bumped!

Practice on a piece of paper first to perfect your technique. Don't worry if you make a mistake—a damp cotton swab will wipe away wet paint.

The "spikes" are weatherproof, so it is not necessary to be delicate, but if you ever need a touch-up, just reapply the paint and let dry.

"I come from major DIY roots—why buy it when you can make it?!"

—JESSICA QUIRK, AUTHOR OF *WHAT I WORE*,
WWW.WHATIWORE.TUMBLR.COM

"I can be a total chameleon when it comes to my style but most days I lean toward classic looks with an edgy twist, like pairing these 'studded' shoes with a more feminine skirt or dress."

—CHRISTINE CAMERON, PERSONAL STYLIST AND FASHION BLOGGER, WWW.MYSTYLEPILL.COM

BRIGHT BOW T-STRAPS

Add a jolt of color to your outfit by knotting bows on your T-straps.

SKILL LEVEL:

WHAT YOU NEED:

2 yd (1.8m) magenta ribbon
Black T-strap heels
Scissors

1. Cut the magenta ribbon into 18 strips, each 4" (10cm) long.

2. Starting from the top, tie the ribbon pieces onto the T-strap with a single knot.

3. Work your way down the strap, using 8–10 pieces of ribbon.

4. After pulling each knot tight, trim the ragged edges with scissors.

Use magenta ribbon if you are looking for high impact, or lower the intensity with a muted tone. Try a gold or silver ribbon for a richer look.

LITTLE BLACK DRESS

The "Little Black Dress,"
or "LBD," is an essential piece
of clothing that will **always and
forever** be in style. From Coco
Chanel's design in the 1920s,
to Audrey Hepburn's iconic LBD
in *Breakfast at Tiffany's*,
to Jackie O.'s and Princess Di's
more conservative versions, this
article of clothing has been worn
in **countless** ways. It's truly the
perfect canvas for DIY,
so I asked fashion insiders how
they would suggest **embellishing**
this wardrobe staple.

"The great thing about a little black dress is that it is a blank slate for a DIY project."

—CINDY WEBER-CLEARY, *INSTYLE* FASHION DIRECTOR

"If you are going to wear a little black dress to a party, find a way to stand out by personalizing it."

—HAL RUBENSTEIN, *INSTYLE* FASHION DIRECTOR

RUFFLED SHOULDERS

Inspired by Jason Wu

THE LOOK

SKILL LEVEL:

✗ ✗ ✗ ✗

WHAT YOU NEED:

Tulle in black and silver
Scissors
Sleeveless black
  dress with medium-
  width straps

GIVE YOUR BASIC BLACK DRESS a makeover and up the "wow" factor by simply tying tulle. The best part is that the transformation is not permanent, so wear your tulle puffs out for a night on the town, then untie them and your LBD remains intact.

1. Fold the black tulle so it is 5" (12.5cm) long and 4 layers thick, and cut.

2. Single-knot the tulle onto the strap of the dress.

3. After the knot is tied tight, fan out the layers of tulle.

4. Repeat with the white tulle. Alternate colors until both straps are covered.

Show off your shoulders by wearing your hair in a high bun, and add a pop of color with bright pink lipstick.

"I find vintage clothing pieces and then go on DIY websites to learn how to alter them— it's really simple."

—OLIVIA MUNN, ACTRESS

EMBELLISHED LBD

Inspired by Erin Fetherston

Create Erin Fetherston's LBD idea with brooches found at your local secondhand store, or make your own pins with buttons and oversize earrings.

SKILL LEVEL:

WHAT YOU NEED:

Decorative buttons or oversize earrings
Superglue
Pin backs
Little black dress

1. Starting with your buttons, simply dab some superglue to the pin back.

2. Adhere the pin back to the back of your button and hold for 10 seconds. (If you are using earrings, bend or cut the post so it is flush with the back of the earring.)

3. Pin your new DIY brooches to your dress as desired.

> "I think the neckline of a little black dress is a great place to add embellishment. You can do anything from adding a cluster of vintage brooches together to create an embellished effect or hand-sew on a grosgrain ribbon in the shape of a bow."

—ERIN FETHERSTON, DESIGNER

MORE LBD IDEAS

"To make it edgy, add studded epaulets; for a bohemian vibe, braid a belt out of silky scarves; and for a pretty look, put lace around the hem or neckline."

—GRETCHEN JONES, DESIGNER
AND *PROJECT RUNWAY* SEASON 8 WINNER

"One of my favorite tricks is to make a few different removable collars to fit the neckline of an ordinary dress. I make a Peter Pan collar in a contrasting color or pattern, a ruffled neckline out of vintage crochet trim, or layers of fringe."

—KEIKO GROVES, DESIGNER OF POSTLAPSARIA
AND FASHION BLOGGER, WWW.KEIKOLYNN.COM

"A great way to add a little embellishment to a basic LBD is to head to your local craft store and purchase three yards of ribbon at least three inches wide for a quick and easy belt."

—KATHRYN FINNEY, AUTHOR AND FOUNDER
WWW.THEBUDGETFASHIONISTA.COM

Finding DIY Inspiration

When I started working in fashion, I was immediately immersed in a world filled with gorgeous clothing, intricate jewelry, celebrity style, and designer looks. Every day I found new inspiration and tried to incorporate what I saw into my wardrobe. Unable to afford the price tag, but well-versed in simple DIY techniques, I began to make my own versions of the tie-dye dresses, friendship bracelets, and grommet and zipper accents coming from designer collections. Giving these styles a personal twist made my outfits unique and allowed me to integrate trends in a way that makes them my own. Now, instead of simply lusting over the latest "it" accessory, I seek out styles that I can reinterpret to suit myself. I find new ideas on the runway, in store windows, magazine ads, and people on the street. I snap photos of anything and everything that sparks an idea. I spend hours wandering the aisles of stores like Home Depot or Michaels to find supplies that will make my next project original and distinctive. When asked where I find inspiration, I know the answer "everywhere" seems vague, but I've found that once you change your thinking from buying to DIYing, you really do see everything around you in a completely new way. My biggest tip is to document it all: take a picture, tear out pages from a magazine, follow runway shows and style blogs online. Create a mood board and tack up all your inspiration. This way, whenever you get the urge to make something, you have a wealth of ideas at your fingertips.

Favorite runway look!

"I get equally inspired by reading fashion blogs and magazines as I do by just going into the craft store. It's good to have a mental stock list of what supplies are easily available to you, so when you get that 'I could make that' feeling, you can act on it."

—JESSICA QUIRK,
AUTHOR OF *WHAT I WORE*,
WWW.WHATIWORE.TUMBLR.COM

Love Kate's style

HOW TO GO FROM FASHION RUNWAY **TO DIY**

Pick your **favorite designers**, go online (I use style.com) and start clicking through the latest season. Start a folder on your desktop, label it "**DIY inspiration**," and begin collecting images of embellished outfits, statement necklaces,and standout shoes. **Focus** on one element and think about how you can make it.

"Absolutely everywhere—
magazines, the Internet,
thrift shops, art, photography,
music, nature, people on the
street, your surroundings.
I love finding inspiration in
unexpected places."
**—KIRSTEN NUNEZ, DIY BLOGGER,
WWW.STUDS-AND-PEARLS.COM**

**Perfect
summer
style**

"Great places to look
for DIY inspiration are
Martha Stewart, Etsy.
com, Craftzine.com,
Designsponge.com,
Instructables.com,
and Craftster.org."
—KUSUM LYNN, STYLIST

"I get my inspiration for DIY from
a whole range of sources: style blogs,
editorials and fashion collections,
as well as on the street! My mind is
always in overdrive trying to work out
how I can DIY a trend or detail that
I see. And with a little perseverance
and imagination I think it's possible to
make anything you see on the runway.
You just need the time!"

**—GENEVA VANDERZEIL, DIY BLOGGER,
WWW.APAIR-ANDASPARE.BLOGSPOT.COM**

"I love to flip through fashion magazines for DIY inspirations. I'm inspired by designer trends I see in magazines. I usually can't afford them, so I'm forced to make them!"

—KRISTEN TURNER, DIY BLOG-GER, WWW.GLITTERGLUE.COM

MY SITES FOR
INSPIRATION

pinterest.com
etsy.com
style.com
instyle.com
mjtrim.com
burdastyle.com
whowhatwear.com
ilovetocreate.com
designsponge.com
projectsinacan.com
michaels.com
glitterguide.com
peoplestylewatch.com
abeautifulmess.typepad.com
apair-andaspare.blogspot.com
stripesandsequins.com
honestlywtf.com
studs-and-pearls.com
lovemaegan.com
psimadethis.com
glitternglue.com
chic-steals.com
dismountcreative.com

"Inspiration can be found anywhere, but for a cornucopia of curated ideas, look to the runways. Make an inspiration board of trends you love and put a twist on them to make them your own."

—KEIKO GROVES, DESIGNER OF POSTLAPSARIA AND FASHION BLOGGER, WWW.KEIKOLYNN.COM

Always in style

Go-To DIY Shopping Spots

For supplies in this book, I love M&J Trimming in New York, and I am a regular at Michaels craft stores, and art supply stores such as Blick Art Materials. For the clothing projects in this book, I used inexpensive secondhand finds to experiment with and found affordable basics at chains such as Kohl's, Target, and H&M.

Blick Art Materials
www.dickblick.com

This art supply store houses all the materials you need to translate art into fashion.

Dollar stores

The seeds of so many DIY ideas can grow with a stop at your local dollar store.

Flea markets

Flea markets are a treasure trove for trinkets such as charms, oversized earrings, brooches, old keys, and lockets. Use these found items to create a necklace or charm bracelet.

Goodwill
www.goodwill.org /get-involved/shop/

What better way to recycle and reuse than shopping secondhand. You will save money, and possibly stumble upon a steal worth bragging about. Mine: Moschino pants (tags still on) for $4.50!

H&M
www.hm.com

A stellar store for on-trend basics that are ideal for customizing.

Hobby Lobby
www.hobbylobby.com

Endless halls of supplies can make all your DIY dreams come true. Many "quick trips" turn into hour-long adventures and armfuls of new projects waiting to be made.

Home Depot
www.homedepot.com

These are the handiest places in town for finding metallic touches for any DIY endeavor. From brackets to bolts, piping to spray paint, home improvement stores have the tools for your next project.

Michaels
www.michaels.com

Located all over the country (even in Manhattan!) and packed with every supply you could possibly need, these stores make DIY accessible to everyone.

M&J Trimming
www.mjtrim.com

This store's walls are lined with every trim under the sun. Fringe, rope, ribbon, jewels; the options are endless. Also great for tassels and Swarovski crystals.

Salvation Army
www.salvationarmyusa.org

Secondhand stores are the best places to find inexpensive clothing to try your projects on.

Target
www.Target.com

Find basics that are affordable. Then bedazzle, dye, or stud them until you make the perfect personalized piece.

"Every town has great flea markets and a Salvation Army to find DIY supplies—you just have to dig!"

—ANNA SUI, FASHION DESIGNER

"I love going to the Army-Navy store because it is so cheap, and you can cut everything up and then put it back together again differently."

—CHRIS BENZ, FASHION DESIGNER

Acknowledgments

Thank you to my family, for listening to me and supporting me through it all. Mom, Dad, Tracey, Sarah, Mike, Mark, Shalini, Kyle, Alex, Nikhil, and little Kashi, you are the best family a girl could have.

To my friends, there are a lot of things in life I could not do without you, and this book is definitely one of them. Now that it is done, we can finally hang out again! Special thanks to Lizzy Carmona for helping me with the words and taking time to tirelessly teach me my alliteration is too much. Thank you all for always believing in me.

To Potter Craft and my editor, Betty Wong, for making this book possible. You found me before I knew DIY would be my next career—thank you for giving it wings.

To *InStyle* and all the amazing people I work with there. I moved to New York to work in magazines. Six months after I got to the city I became an intern at *InStyle*, and four years later I had my own DIY column in the magazine. You molded my career and I will forever be grateful. Thank you.

To Jamie Beck, your photographs are breathtaking, and you and Kevin Burg's cinemagraphs will make history. You both are an absolute pleasure to work with. Thank you for making the already gorgeous ladies in this book look stunning.

To my models: Jessica Quirk, Christine Cameron, Kim Pesch, and Alison Dahl. You are all phenomenal. I want to thank you and your websites for being constant sources of inspiration. Your friendship and guidance through the book and blogging world is invaluable.

To all the designers, stylists, and fashionable people who contributed tips and projects, thank you for making this book extra special.

Thank you Club Monaco and Coach for lending us the clothes and bags that made the photo shoots complete.

A huge thank you to the DIY and fashion blogger community. I had no idea that making things and sharing them with others could be a career. Thanks to you I get to wake up every morning and do something I love.

Photo Credits

Pages 20: Arnold Turner/WireImage/Getty Images; Page 24: Han Myung-Gu/WireImage/Getty Images; Page 28: Steve Granitz/WireImage/Getty Images; Page 32: Stephen Lovekin/Getty Images Entertainment/Getty Images; Page 38: Michael Caulfield/Getty Images Entertainment/Getty Images; Page 44: Donato Sardella/WireImage/Getty Images; Page 50: Karl Prouse/Catwalking/Getty Images; Page 54: Chris Moore/Catwalking/Getty Images; Page 60: Jemal Countess/Getty Images Entertainment/Getty Images; Page 64: Karl Prouse/Catwalking/WireImage/Getty Images; Page 70: Frazer Harrison/Getty Images Entertainment/Getty Images; Page 74: Thomas Concordia/WireImage/Getty Images; Page 82: John Kobal Foundation/Moviepix/Getty Images; Page 88: Silver Screen Collection/Moviepix/Getty Images; Page 92: Everett Collection/Rex USA/BEImages; Page 98: John Kobal Foundation/Moviepix/Getty Images; Page 146: Slaven Vlasic/Getty Images Entertainment/Getty Images; Page 102: Don Cravens/TIME & LIFE Images/Getty Images; Page 152: (top) Frazer Harrison/Getty Images Entertainment/Getty Images; (bottom) Chris Moore/Catwalking/Getty Images; Page 153: (clockwise from top left) Slaven Vlasic/Getty Images Entertainment/Getty Images; Arnold Turner/WireImage/Getty Images; Karl Prouse/Catwalking/WireImage/Getty Images; Han Myung-Gu/WireImage/Getty Images

About the Author

Growing up in the Midwest, **Jenni Radosevich** was determined to create her own style. If she saw something in a magazine that she couldn't find in her local department store, she would make the look herself. Working at *InStyle*, Jenni has become part of the industry she always admired. Her affinity for creating current "looks for less" has manifested into a column for the magazine and a website, www.ISpy-DIY.com. She lives in New York City.

Index

Note: Page numbers in **bold** indicate projects.